Big and Small Animals

by Ann Corcorane

Consultant:
Adria F. Klein, Ph.D.
California State University, San Bernardino

capstone
classroom

Heinemann Raintree • Red Brick Learning
division of Capstone

This cat is big.

These cats are small.

These horses are big.

This horse is small.

This bird is big.

This bird is small.

Elephants are big and small.